Somehow, here

poems by

Katherine Dizon

Finishing Line Press
Georgetown, Kentucky

Somehow, here

ACKNOWLEDGMENTS

With gratitude to all the editors of the following journals where these
poems, sometimes in earlier forms or with different titles, were first
published:

Clover: When There Were Fireworks (previously called July 4, 2007)
Common Ground Review: Ars Poetica (I am a letter)
Creative Colloquy: Doesn't Every Poet Write a Poem About Spring
Cleaning?, Still Awake
Flora Fiction: We Were the Only Two Who Wrote About Each Other
Gold Man Review: The Time-Space Continuum
HoosierLit: Dear First Love
Silver Rose Magazine: Wicker Park, Chicago: Twelve Years Since We've
   Seen Each Other

Publisher: Leah Huete de Maines
Editor: Christen Kincaid
Cover Art: Matthew Dizon
Author Photo: Michael Dizon
Cover Design: Elizabeth Maines McCleavy

Order online: www.finishinglinepress.com
         also available on amazon.com

Author inquiries and mail orders:
Finishing Line Press
PO Box 1626
Georgetown, Kentucky 40324
USA

Contents

Until you have loved,
you cannot become yourself.
—Emily Dickinson

Sunflowers

I didn't expect them to grow.
Pack of seeds I found
buried in my bedside table drawer,
which I planted late fall
inside a cement block
in front of the house, scattered
and covered the seeds with rocky dirt,
the ground already hardening.
The rain came.
One day, pulling into the driveway
I noticed a flash of yellow through the grey.
There, two sunflowers, only inches high,
who rose even though their season
was long past. It cheered me to see them
out the window of my daughter's room,
or when I'd step outside to get the mail.

I smiled to see that pair of flowers,
even though I knew in the dark it was wrong,
that they didn't stand a chance against the winter.
So much work must have happened
before I even saw them, such strength
unnoticed, green shoots pressing through earth,
reaching toward sky into a world not ready for them—
but how could they know that?
They didn't choose where or when to exist,

any more than I chose him or the way
we found each other at different times
in our lives, bursting into the briefest bloom.

Ars Poetica

Childhood summers playing pool in my cousin's basement,
　　　I could never sink the eight ball if I aimed directly
for it. Instead, periphery. I learned the verb ricochet.

*

With every shake of a snow globe, the orb clouds and then
　　　clears. I watch as tiny glittering flakes settle, never the
same way twice, but who can tell? No wonder tears can mean
　　　sadness, or not.

*

It's quiet, the silent space between words, what's left to my
　　　imagination. I paint with that silence, bright brilliant
hues. Every night, Northern Lights. Colors of what we could
　　　have been.

Doesn't Every Poet Write a Poem about Spring Cleaning?

Lately I've noticed red buds
at the tips of tree branches
in front of our house;
birds huddled in groups
in grassy fields and leafless trees,
swapping stories of their winter travels;
the sun lingering a little more
with each evening sky.

And inside,
I've been cleaning house,
choosing what stays and goes.

These cookbooks I took years ago
from my grandmother's house,
but they really could have come from
a used bookstore: they do not contain
her handwriting, or any meals I can recall
her making, or any recipes I've tried myself.
These can go.

These aprons I never wear, but seemed
like the kind of thing a married woman,
and mother, ought to have in her kitchen.
Instead of the colorful, handmade ones
I've received over the years from family,
the one I hold onto is black, from Plum Market,
where I worked as a cashier the year
we were engaged.

Some objects are easy to toss,
too broken, too dirty, or too old to keep around:
a green body pillow from college,
the cheap floor lamp that always leaned,
two high chair feeding seats,
the stroller I backed over one day and bent,
bibs with stains that never came out.

We've been married almost eight years now
and moved seven times, carrying with us
the same taped-up boxes and plastic tubs,
some we haven't opened for years: their contents
long forgotten.

I didn't even notice I'd also brought with me,
unchanged by time or distance, the memories
of my first love. Somehow, here
and now I've unpacked them
and need to decide where they go,
because they can't stay.
There is no shelf suitable for display,
and even the closet or garage
feels too close.

But how is one ever ready to toss those moments
away, alongside the old bank statements
and magazines and clothes that don't fit?
For now, I let my hands close around this one:

it's twenty-degrees and snowy
in a small college town in Indiana
where I lay beside him in the dark quiet hours,
my head on his chest, his arm holding
me close, finding warmth in each other,

before there was any need for spring.

We Were the Only Two Who Wrote About Each Other

first day of winter writing class
first time living somewhere with winter
the snow clumped on tree branches
felt like a new nostalgia

choose a stranger in the room
five minutes to compose a poem
he wore navy blue turtleneck
khaki pants legs crossed
staring across the room
at me curly blonde with glasses
a watch too big that kept sliding up my arm
we shared glances between lines

unfamiliar terrain outside and in
freshly fallen snow on the ground
more to come, dark sky weighted
with moisture cold enough to crystallize
all the words we had yet to speak

after class he crossed the room
to talk to me, first flakes
perfect conditions to fall
keep falling

if only I could rewrite the rest the mess
the way it melted so fast revealing
dirt that had always been there

I could not have known how that cold
would hunker down, hibernate in my body
follow me back to the west coast
where years later I'd awaken one spring
a married mother to find the cold still there
still burned all the parts of me I'd left exposed

Nostalgia

Septembers seem to come faster now,
cold compression of fall into holidays.
How can it still surprise me,
newly crisp morning and evening air,

the sun's sudden shyness?
The faster the changes come,
the further I feel myself traveling
in time from those I've lost,

including my selves. Decades ago,
half a country and lifetime
from where I am now–
where apples are the state fruit

and yet, it's rare to find a place
where you can pick them,
where they grow wild–
I visited for the first time a new land:

an *apple orchard*, in Mooresville, Indiana,
with trees cloaked in their full regalia—
colors of cornsilk and cedar chest,
tumbleweed and rose dust—

and inside the Apple Barn, I tasted,
atop a hot fried biscuit, *apple butter*,
which is less butter and more sauce,
both sweet and sour, imbued

with seasonal spices–cinnamon,
cloves, nutmeg. Freshly simmered
with all that Midwestern warmth.
That was back when sweets

could be savored, not saved. I could eat
anything. Life still full of first times.
The future a seed I did not know
where to plant, or what would grow.

When There Were Fireworks

I believed the writer giving his book talk on the second
floor of Books & Co. in Dayton, Ohio when he said he'd
figured out how to time travel.

I remember only scraps of his story–New York City,
when he was a young boy, his father was murdered—
so he spent his life learning how to go back, find more time.

Forget the fact that this took place in the bulls-eye
of a shopping center and that Ohio is a state I never could
quite remember where it stood in the great center of things

or that this claim, if real, is something news sources
might have picked up on. It felt like we'd stumbled
upon some important secret meant for us alone.

The author's name or his book title, both lost now
in that great rushing river of my mind. I've spent hours
searching lists of time travel books, reading theories,

news stories, scientific gains, but none connected me
to that bookstore on July 4, 2007, nothing could confirm
this memory was real. So, maybe he was successful,

slipped away without anyone noticing, traveled back,
changed his future, no need to author a book on time
travel, found more years to spend with his father,

found what he'd spent his whole life searching for.
I want that time machine to take me back to that day,
show me the way I looked to the young man I sat beside

in that bookstore, how close our legs were to touching
in our chairs, whether later that night I was beside him
on the blanket at RiverScape park when the sky darkened

without our noticing, then suddenly exploded in bursts
of light and color, the entire fireworks display all at once
before the storm reached us, barely enough time for us

to run back to the car through drenching rain, time to tell me
as I sat laughing and shivering in the car what I didn't know then:
how he saw me, how he wanted to disappear into forever with me.

Ars Poetica

For years I stopped writing
and inside me all those words,
trapped without escape, began
their slow, unseen decay.
Meanwhile, from the outside,
I was living.

Usually, by the time heart rot
disease is found in a tree,
it's too late to save it. No one
noticed when the fungus
entered through exposed
wounds. It could have been
months, or years, while
the infection spread,
slowly consuming the center,
weakening the inside,
a wonder it's still standing.

Sometimes, a tree can contain
the invader, prevent it from
hollowing the heartwood.
Then, it's possible to remove
the afflicted limb, leave the rest,
hope the fungus won't return.
But for most—if too much time
has passed, the disease progressed—
before it collapses, before it crashes
through the living room wall,
before it falls and takes down
everything and everyone with it,
you know what needs to be done.

Pick up the axe, chop down the tree,
tear out the roots, plant what you can,
begin the difficult work of waiting,
tending and trusting what moves
in the dark. You cannot know
what will grow but this new life
is not the old one.
It is stronger. It remembers.

On Flight

I've heard that memory works like a library,
where we approach the circulation desk
and ask for a book, which sometimes is there
or not. Sometimes, we're offered a substitute,
one we hadn't thought to ask for.

How can I tell you, dear reader, about a day
I saw butterflies released without sounding
cliché? Without you feeling clobbered
with intended meaning? I'll try, anyway:

it happened during college years, on one
of my visits to the school I'd left, with D and
our complicated history. The setting, our
poetry professor's house on Seminary Street.

Let's say we ran into him earlier that day
on campus. Let's say he told us we should
come by later to see the release of his daughter's
butterflies she'd been raising. No, let's say

the event was unexpected: D and I were walking
through the neighborhood and stopped by to say hi,
and our professor invited us in, and the librarian
of my mind has only retrieved for me fragments,

a hallway and dark brown wood of a stair railing.
We're ushered into a cozy kitchen with a breakfast
nook and on the counter we see a cylindrical net,
just like the one I'll get in the future with my own kids

because this memory will live inside me, and I'll want
to pass it on. D and I follow them to their back porch,
my professor and his daughter who slowly, carefully,
unzip the top of the netted home of five butterflies

who arrived as caterpillars in the mail three weeks ago,
who need coaxing to freedom, who don't at first notice
the opening. What must it be like, their first encounter
with a flower, first taste of wild geranium, vanilla scent

of Sweet Joe Pye Weed? Maybe they're overwhelmed,
drunk with happiness, but I know this is only one
backyard at the edge of the world and already they're
leaving, beyond the tulip poplars rimming the grass.

We watch them rise higher and higher, until they've gone
to find more flowers and fields, as far and fully as their
wings will carry them, and who were we to witness this
first flight? Dear reader, if you're expecting me

to say that I was the butterfly, you wouldn't be wrong.
But now, turning this borrowed book over in my hands,
I find myself looking away from the sky and instead,
at the father and his daughter. Perhaps, it wasn't a daughter,

but a son. Perhaps, at that time, his children were already grown
and moved out of the house. Maybe, he'd been by
his front door for years, waiting for us to come back,

to remind us there's a universe beyond what we can see,
beyond what we've ever allowed ourselves to dream or ask for.

Excavate

I wasn't looking for it, but I've kept what's written, more permanent than memory. I was reading through journals, like an amnesiac, desperate. Tucked between pages, the letter. When I held it, it wasn't my brain but my body that remembered. Reacted. Cream-colored envelope speckled red and black, no name on the outside, the flap an asymmetrical triangle, never sealed. Or, what kept it closed once had worn away. Inside, matching stationary, one night's words fossilized on paper folded twice with precision. How does the paleontologist know she's touched the last bone? Or, the start of a new skeleton? He'd written *Katherine*, my formal name, both close and distant, the way he was. The way we were. His words obsidian, slicing the fragile story I'd told myself. He signed his apologies *with love (accepted or not)*. That's when I learned time doesn't heal wounds. It seals them. Container of pain, still pulsing.

U-Turn

Everything has shifted here in Greencastle, Indiana: Starbucks at
the town square diagonal from the German V-1 buzz bomb perched

on a V for victory in front of the courthouse, which you can't help
but notice as it's right in the center of everything, and you almost

feel like you're walking on a movie set for any small town America.
Across the street is the pharmacy which I remember was small, with

carpet, where I could buy a hot dog from the same window where I
picked up my birth control pills, but the pharmacy's been replaced by

a tourist information stop where I pick up brochures of this vaguely
familiar place from another decade when another me went to college

a few blocks away. The coffee shop Gathering Grounds is now a real
estate office and other blooming establishments include an ice cream

shop and a craft brewery. Still there is Marv's, with walls covered in
photographs taken from travelers and concert-goers grinning holding

signs like "Marvin's delivers to Sheryl Crow," and I can remember
them delivering my 10 p.m. order to my sorority house, their specialty

GCB, garlic cheeseburger, which I've found replicated nowhere, thick
patty between a hoagie roll powdered with garlic. The best ketchup's

ever tasted was with that burger dipped corner by corner into it and
now it tastes just the same. As I walk campus, I keep thinking smaller,

smaller, smaller, the memories that loomed so large have shrunk now
that I'm looking right at them. The library cafe is closed, the chairs

look worn, the lighting dim. In Asbury Hall, I squint at the classroom
trying to see the circle of desks, the day we met, the day I looked

down that road as far as I could. The pond I remember frozen in winter in the center quad on campus is disappeared, grass grown

in its place as if always. The Thompson Recital Hall shortcut I'd take to keep warm is gone, I'm disoriented standing in a doorway

where I remember it, but the inner hallway has moved along with the piano practice rooms and I have to ask a current student where

the pianos are, find out down a set of new stairs, the original red brick walls beside new white stucco, and now I'm here at the keys,

expecting magic, for my hands to remember a song that they don't. Some things lost forever, as if one of the ancient glaciers

that shaped this state has flattened my own life, buried and crushed everything, and now it's retreating, now it's melting, now

it's spilling rivers in all directions.

Still Awake

golden shovel, after Mary Oliver

Some nights I wish you had never learned my
name, that instead we'd been strangers whose shoulders
brushed on a red line train, before we emerged from the covered
station into the city's lights, the contact unnoticed, with
darkness to disappear us, remaining as wordless as stars.

Ars Poetica

can be like the time I went hiking alone
outside Dublin, in my 20s with a few days
to fill before my studies started in London,

and wanted to see the sea. I started on
a dirt path overlooking Dublin Bay,
when I noticed two middle-aged men

walking the trail a distance behind me.
Alone in a foreign country, I picked up
my pace, hoped I'd lose them, thought

I did, until, as I rested on a bench, they
appeared from around a curve, said
how fast I'd walked, and began

making small talk, which I avoid,
especially in other countries. I can't
explain it, but we ended up walking

the rest of the trail together, not far,
and when they asked me to join them
for a beer at the pub where the trail ends,

I found myself saying yes, and they
introduced me to a shandy: beer with
lemon soda, beer for non-beer-drinkers.

That could have been good enough, little
poem-in-your-pocket, meeting these
harmless friends from Liverpool,

getting back to sight-seeing in Dublin
on my own, but they invited me to more.
An annual horse race on a beach,

that only happens one day in September
when the tide is low. By that point,
I trusted them, and, still knowing the risks,

joined them in a taxi to the beach
and crowds and speed and cheering,
saw a racehorse up close, walked

beside these two men who never
made me feel uncomfortable, but
rather cared for, like two fathers,

who, on the train back to Dublin,
gave me their phone numbers,
which I kept in a scrapbook of my

travels, said if I was ever in Liverpool,
to call them, they'd remember me,
and I said I would, and meant it,

even cheek-kissed them goodbye
at my stop, and knew that's why
I do this: to remember and be

remembered, knowing sometimes
going in I'll find danger and pain,
but also surprise and delight, and,

either way, always come out
the other side, very much alive.

The Time-Space Continuum

I've found the wormhole, Mr. Hawking,
while you were still thinking
about your party for time travelers
when no one arrived.
On one end is snow
on the other, evergreens:
the years between stretched
just large enough for me to pass through.

Should we consult science or poetry
to understand the way I traveled,
still unable to free myself
from the gravity of his words?

I did not predict we'd keep writing,
our words reaching across time
and space, creating a kind of room
where we leave them, where he and I visit,
but never together. By the time
I read his next letter, he is already gone.
As I stay to write mine, only echoes.

We speak and wait for answers.
Any moment the tunnel could collapse,
a dying star dragging everything
around it into the abyss—
my husband, two children, this self
I barely recognize—
yet I shiver, remembering

his touch, tender fingers
curling my hair behind my ear
as I lay with my head in his lap
while some movie plays for us alone.
Knowing even then it wouldn't last.

Dear First Love

I did not know
white deer existed
until I saw them
in the large meadow
I always drive past
on the way out of town.

At first I thought I'd imagined them
but then wanted to know,
What is the word for that?

Not albino, or leucistic,
but piebald, since their
heads and tails are brown—
but these words do not
satisfy me.

What I really want to know is:
where do the deer go,
when they don't return
to the grassland
for weeks at a time?

I'd like to disappear
with them one day,
follow them back
into the evergreen forest
at the base of the rocky hill.
I imagine we'd weave
through trees, emerge
in a faraway field,
Ohio maybe, or Illinois.

You'd be there too,
waiting
for the same deer to return,

wondering where they go
when they're away,
searching for the right words
to explain why you can't
forget them,
not knowing
why there had to be
so many years
of silence.

But that's foolishness, of course.
There are no more roads that lead to you.

Only these piebald deer, who appear
without pattern or prediction,
white flash in the field
as I drive by, toward every
predictable place.

At Benedict Inn Monastery

While the nuns recite
their evening prayers
I'm alone outside
in the gazebo
watching lightning bugs.

Their random blinking,
a dozen tiny lighthouses
rolling in my vision.
How could anyone
look away from this light?

I returned to Indiana
hoping to remember
why I spent so much of my life
chasing lightning bugs, believing
when I caught one
it would somehow change
        anything.

It was easy to blame
the timing,
something beyond our control.
Why couldn't I see
that while I moved towards one,
it was already
        moving away?

I follow the light,
cup my hands around one.
How small it really is,
each black wing like a sunflower seed—
a disappointment from the promise
        of its glow.

But it wasn't even about him, really.
Or any of them.

All along it was me, firefly
of the west, faintly flashing,
barely visible in the dark,

just wanting
to be found,
for someone
to follow
the staccato
of my call.

Wicker Park, Chicago: Twelve Years Since We've Seen Each Other

Today, a surprise snowstorm
in April, after sunny and 70s,
just in time for our re-meeting.
The snow falls
as stinging rain, freezing
our faces as we trudge
between restaurants
and bookshops,
neighborhoods he knows.
Nothing sweet, or soft.
The wind howls.
We don't talk
as we walk. Crossing streets
he moves on ahead,
does not offer me his elbow
does not look back
to see I've made it safely around
the expanses of water off curbs.
Inside The Wormhole,
he orders me Earl Grey tea.
He drinks espresso while we sit
apart on a couch, close enough
to hear our fits and starts
of conversation over the hum
of strangers around us.
We were 80s babies,
grew up with what's around us:
Ghostbusters and *Indiana Jones*
movie posters, classic Nintendo,
computer monitor the size of
a mini fridge, and above us,
a reconstructed DeLorean,
traveling to no future.
Drifting on the once infinite sea
of things to say,
we are nearing shore,
where it looks dry, and warm.

Ars Poetica

I'm a letter
without need

for response,
a letter between

friends, old friends,
the kind of friend

I had when
I was young,

young enough
not to hide,

when I lived
wide open

to a world
that would break

my heart,
a heart I thought

knew breaking before,
but hadn't.

I am a bowl
mended by kintsugi,

a whole
made of pieces

broken and fused
together, golden

repair. A stained-
glass window

that fractures
light.

I am apology
and I am forgiveness,

a penance
for the pain

we inflict
and pass on,

a lifetime
of Hail Marys

and hallelujahs,
no longer mine

to carry alone.
I shine

when I find air,
when I join you.

January Light

Desolation

in the land without
                              ocean,
                    without my bearings.
Deep winter, negative degrees,
snowpack and train tracks
                    that ran along the outside

of campus, to destinations
                              unknown. It was hard to see,
                    then, by light
                    unreflected by ocean blues.
I felt my way through the dim, thin haze.

Found consolation

                              in poetry and *Il Postino*,
                    images of oceans (that churned up
inside me the sick for home way I felt)
                    and Pablo Neruda,
Oda a la Manzana, ode to this apple,
                              ode to that lamp, ode
                    to a professor who wore black turtlenecks
                    (really)
who said: *Write something
                    no one has written before.*

Is that even possible?

                    We all begin with language,
                    first felt in the body
and then let loose through our lips,
          as sounds
                              then words
made of letters
                    huddling together in the cold:
little airplanes of meaning

assembled and sent out
on the runway.

We share this:
A painter, their paints.
A musician, their notes.

I keep trying to do what you said,
move the letters around,
pick them up with fingertips
and set them down, just so.
Sometimes, I scoop
with both hands,
throw them against the wall
and watch them fall.

*What no one's written
is what only you can write.*

I used to walk campus alone at night,
especially that winter, Narnian lamp posts
lining the paved paths. Sometimes,
I ended up at the stadium,
sat in the bleachers overlooking
the spot-lighted field, empty,
breathed in the smell of salt in the air,
listened for the resonance of seashells.

Now, wherever I find myself,
when winter arrives,
when the airplanes are grounded,
waiting to be de-iced,
I can slip inside my very own wardrobe of coats,
emerge into a 2nd floor classroom,
corner of Vine and Seminary Streets,
where a bonfire's embers
still glow, incandescent,
deep in the heart of it all.

NOTES

- The title "Doesn't Every Poet Write a Poem about Spring Cleaning?" came from Mary Oliver's poem titled "Doesn't Every Poet Write a Poem about Unrequited Love?"

- The poem "Ars Poetica (Childhood summers)" was selected for the Longlist of the Letter Review Prize for Poetry.

Katherine Dizon grew up in the San Francisco Bay Area and has lived most of her adult life in Washington State, with brief stays in Indiana, Michigan, and Connecticut. Her poems have appeared in journals such as *Common Ground Review, Creative Colloquy, Gold Man Review, Cirque,* and *Clover.* She has a BA in Creative Writing and MAT in Elementary Education from University of Puget Sound, and MFA in Poetry from the Rainier Writing Workshop at Pacific Lutheran University. Katherine is devoted to her three beautiful children and her cat, Dexter. She's grateful to her partner, Matthew, for being her constant. Katherine enjoys traveling, seeing live theatre and music concerts, and finding peace and joy in nature. She received poor grades in science in school, but is inspired to explore it in her poetry.

www.ingramcontent.com/pod-product-compliance
Lightning Source LLC
Chambersburg PA
CBHW022053080426
42734CB00009B/1331